Integrating Data

Bill Inmon

Patty Haines

David Rapien

Technics Publications

115 Linda Vista

Sedona, AZ 86336 USA

https://www.TechnicsPub.com

Edited by Jamie Hoberman

Cover design by Lorena Molinari

First Printing 2022

Copyright © 2022 by Bill Inmon, Patty Haines, and David Rapien

ISBN, print ed.   9781634622820
ISBN, Kindle ed. 9781634622837
ISBN, ePub ed.   9781634622844
ISBN, PDF ed.   9781634622868

Library of Congress Control Number: 2022941429

Contents

Introduction

What are the essential processes that take place within a data warehouse? Possibly the most important is the integration of data. Integration provides the organization with the same unified view of data. Unfortunately, despite the benefit of integration, nobody wants to *do* the integration. Everyone hates integration, including vendors, data analysts, data scientists, and consultants. So why do people hate data integration so much?

People hate integration because integration requires thought and work—a lot of thought and a lot of work. There are no shortcuts.

A typical vendor tactic is to provide users with a platform and then put the responsibility of integration on these users. Often this process is called Extract, Load, and Transform (ELT). And what happens when ELT is set into motion? Due to ELT complexity, often integration conveniently does not get done.

E and L get done, but we forget about T.

The problem is that you must integrate the data to have a truly unified view of data across the enterprise. There are no shortcuts. There are no easy paths out.

So what do you end up with when you do not integrate data? You have a world of silos of information. One silo cannot communicate or cooperate with another silo. Data exists solely within its silo and you cannot use it anywhere else. You have no way of looking at information across the enterprise.

We must integrate all sorts of data: structured, transaction-based, and textual data. There is a lot of important data within the organization that we overlook today. And that is a shame because organizations are missing a great opportunity. Organizations need to look at all of their data, not just the data that is convenient to use.

There have been many unsuccessful trends in avoiding data integration:

- Just build a data mart from applications using the dimensional model. Who needs all the work of building a data warehouse? Go directly from application to data mart and skip all data integration work using dimensional modeling.

- Let's change the definition of a data warehouse. And in doing so, not do integration because it is hard and complex.

- Let's do ELT rather than ETL. Only let's skip the T part of the equation.

- Let's copy operational data into a separate platform and call it "integrated data." That is a lot simpler than getting in there and unifying the data.

- Let's bring in big data. I heard that with big data we didn't really have to integrate our data. The vendor told us that if we just put all of our data into big data, we would not need a data warehouse.

- Let's do a data mesh. Who needs all the complications of integration?

- Let's just put everything in a data lake. Then people can go to the data lake and just find what they want. That's all there is to it.

Every day, vendors create more excuses not to do integration. And every day, the problems with siloed systems grow worse.

If you want to create corporate, believable data out of your corporation, you must integrate the data out of your silos.

We integrate data at three levels:

- Semantic
- Metadata
- Operational

The techniques for data integration are very different for classical structured data versus textual data. Integration with structured data involves a data model, whereas integration with text involves a taxonomy and other mappings, ontologies, and inline contextualization. And these different tools that support integration are very different from each other.

There are (at least) two important aspects to integration. The first aspect is the mechanics of integration, and the second aspect is the project management of integration. This book covers both of these aspects.

Vendors and consultants fear integration. The first step to not fearing integration is to understand it. Once you understand integration, you can rationally start to plan how to do integration.

Bill Inmon/Denver, Colorado

Patty Haines/Denver, Colorado

David Rapien/Cincinnati, Ohio

CHAPTER 1

Integration

If one subject is universally disliked in the world of technology, it is the subject of integrating data. Vendors hate integration. Consultants hate integration. End-users hate integration. Once data arrives in a silo of data, it never comes out.

Data arrives in the corporation from many sources. Once the data exists in digital form, the analyst/end-user believes the data. It is a shock to the end-user that the data they are using is incorrect. And the end-user finds that it is very difficult to make informed decisions on unreliable data.

So what kind of data is subject to the many different inaccuracies that plague data in the corporation? The answer is – all kinds of data are subject to inaccuracy.

Inaccuracy of data

There are many reasons for data inaccuracy, such as entering, calculating, or copying data incorrectly.

Lack of integration

But the biggest cause of inaccurate, unbelievable data is the lack of proper integration across the enterprise. When data is not integrated, it is entered into one location and can't be used in another. Usually, unintegrated data exists in large silos of information. These silos of information allow data to be used and understood only within the context of the silo. The moment data steps outside of the silo, it loses context and meaning.

For example, in a large corporation, a person wants to find out information about a customer for automobiles. The analyst enters one system looking for the customer and finds nothing. Then the analyst enters another system for people who buy tires and finds someone with a similar name. But it isn't the right person. Then the analyst enters yet another system and finds the right person, and it only has data on gasoline purchases. But gasoline purchases are for much smaller amounts than an automobile. By this time, the customer had left and found another dealership and the analyst forgot why they were looking.

Not finding accurate data quickly and easily has very negative consequences.

There is much value in having an enterprise view of accurate and complete data. And this is true for all organizations.

The problem is that integrating data is difficult and complex. Integrating requires hard work and sleuth investigation. Integration requires making mistakes and correcting them. However, integrating data is absolutely necessary to achieve a true enterprise view of data.

You cannot have an enterprise view of data as long as the data is not integrated.

There are no shortcuts. There are no alternatives. There are no silver bullets. There are no easy paths out.

So how did data ever get to be so messed up?

1. We design applications with no thought of integration. We build each application with its own symbology, names, calculations, and encoding algorithms. When the application was built, no thought was ever given to any standardization across the enterprise.

2. There is much data in the form of text. When people write and talk, they don't speak in terms of integrated terms, keys, or attributes. Such a conversation would sound very unusual indeed.

But these conversations still hold tremendous value to the corporation.

3. Organizations change, merge, and split apart. One day a system is aligned with another system that was once a competitor. We never planned for these systems to be integrated, so it is no surprise that the systems don't fit together.

4. Time passes and business changes. There are new laws, new competitors, and new economic conditions. If there is one immutable law of nature, that law is that over time, business conditions change. And this law is true for all businesses.

5. There are mentality silos. When managers make decisions, they rarely look across departments because they are using their budget for their department. They don't want to take money from their employees to give it to someone else. Let someone else fund integration. Most of us understand our jobs only in relation to our work area. Accountants understand accounting, taxes, audits, and rules. Marketing people understand sales, commissions, marketing campaigns, and advertising. Operations managers understand manufacturing, supply chain and queuing theory. Data analysts understand data and sometimes

statistics. Developers understand code and data structures.

6. There is near-sightedness. Not many developers have studied or worked in Marketing, Accounting, or Operations. So, when they design the systems, tables, attributes, and data storage, there is no need to consider integration with the rest of the organization. Often, they do not even understand the jobs of the department for whom they are writing the software. Even within the silo, they often do not personally interact with the real end-users. Instead, they have some manager who is a go between. Data analysts are often handcuffed with similar constraints. The results of new systems being developed within the silos are good for the singular task(s), but detrimental to the integration of organization-wide data.

7. People don't like change. Organizations often build or acquire their software to achieve a particular task. They depend on this software to run their departments. The employees become trained and familiar with the software and people do not like change. As a result, we become more reliant on these systems and they become unchangeable and indispensable. The problem is that the organization is now at the complete mercy of the consultants or software providers.

8. People like power. Organizations often purchase large MRP, ERP, or other vendor packages to run their businesses. We are sold a system that promises to be all things to all people across all departments. The salespeople demonstrate a high level of marketing, finance, accounting, and ops integration. They sell us on best-of-breed and comprehensive reporting. What is often not shown or talked about is that they have built their application from buying many disparate systems that do not natively talk to each other or share integrated databases. So, when we ask for our organization-wide and integrated reports, they come with a caveat that "we have that report in our production list". The system replaced our legacy systems and now we cannot get out from under their power.

The only difference from one business to the next is the rate and scope of change. But business changes all the time. It simply is a fact that one day the organization awakes to find that there is no integrated view of data in the corporation. And this lack of integration puts management in a precarious position. Not having integrated corporate enterprise data is like flying an airplane in the clouds without instrumentation. It is just a matter of time before a disaster occurs.

Integrated data allows us to answer basic and important questions as:

- How many customers do we have?
- What products do we have?
- What revenue do we have?
- Are we growing? Or are we losing customers?
- Are we maintaining customer loyalty?

Running a business without being able to answer these basic questions is very difficult to do.

What is needed is corporate data (or enterprise data), not application data or data gathered in a conversation.

The challenge of data integration is that it is complex in the best of cases and bewildering in the worst of cases.

Many organizations decide not to integrate their data due to the high level of complexity and effort.

Spider web systems

What happens to organizations that decide not to integrate their systems? Ultimately the organization ends up with a "spider web" environment.

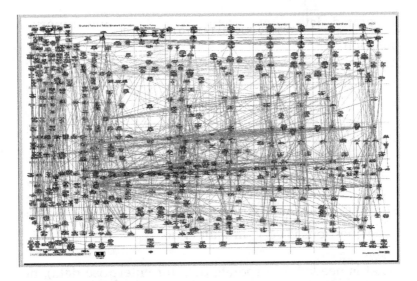

Figure 1-1. In the spider web environment, applications and extract programs toss data from one application to the next. Soon there will be many extract programs connecting many applications.

So what is so terrible about a spider web architecture?

There are lots of things wrong with the spider web architecture:

- **Lack of data integrity**. In a spider web environment no one knows the actual value of any given element of data. The data ends up being shuffled around from one application to the next through the process of extraction. The result is that the same attribute ends up existing in multiple places. The problem is that the attribute has a different value in all the places in which it exists. In one place, the attribute has a value of 650. In another place the attribute has a value of 5000. In another place the attribute has the value of 50.

- **Inability to find the real value of an attribute**. Not only are attributes scattered around like leaves in the fall time, but the data cannot be reconciled. In other words, finding an attribute's actual value is very difficult, if not impossible.

- **Difficult to fix**. It is challenging to repair the spider web environment. Most managers add hardware, software, and consultants to solve the problems of the spider web environment. This makes the spider web environment even worse.

- **Easier to ignore textual data**. What happens to a corporation when it ignores its textual data? The organization is ignoring 90% of its information. This includes the voice of the customer, corporate contracts with all of their liability, and warranty fulfillment which can improve the manufacturing process by understanding defective parts, insurance claims processing, and medical records.

The net result of an organization not integrating their data and ignoring textual data is that the organization is flying its airplane in the clouds with no instrumentation. When that happens, it is a short time until disaster strikes. Stated another way, when an organization integrates its structured data and incorporates its textual data, the organization ends up being in a proactive position. Once an organization finds itself in a proactive position, it can anticipate customers and adjust to changing market conditions.

Reasons for complexity

There are many reasons for the complexity the analyst uncovers when integrating data.

For structured data:

- There is no documentation of what data in a system means
- There is documentation, but it is out of date
- The only documentation is in old code in a language that no one uses or understands anymore
- Documentation of systems must be done at several levels
- The semantic level
- The physical level
- The inclusion/exclusion level
- The calculation level

For textual data:

- Different languages must be accounted for
- Slang must be taken into account
- Misspellings must be considered

- The context of text must be understood
- The dialects of language must be taken into consideration

Of all of these considerations, the most important is the context of text. You need context to understand what is being said. Merely trying to decipher and understand text by itself is simply not adequate. Instead, we must consider text and context when integrating text into a database.

Transformation of data

In its simplest form, integration is nothing more than data transformation. We transform data from application data to corporate data or text to corporate data. The data is then in a singular and integrated state, creating a true organizational picture.

The challenge with context is that it is normally found outside of the text.

To understand what is meant by context existing outside of text, consider the following simple example:

Two men are talking about a lady, and one says to the other, "She's hot."

Now, what is meant by "she's hot."

One possibility is that he finds the lady attractive. Another possibility is that it is Houston, Texas in July, and the lady is sweating and physically hot. A third possibility is that the men are doctors. One doctor has just taken her temperature, and she has a temperature of 104 degrees Fahrenheit. In addition, she has a fever and is internally hot.

To make sense of the words "she's hot," you need to know:

Are the men doctors?

Is the conversation occurring in Houston, Texas in July?

Do they find the lady attractive?

Those factors are external to the text, "She's hot." To understand the context, you must know many things that are not directly related to the spoken or written text. The external factors allow the words to have meaning.

The understanding of the external context of the words allows the words to be understood.

Trying to understand the context by looking internally (spoken word), will not lead to a proper interpretation of what is being said. And without a proper interpretation, it is impossible to properly integrate the text into the corporation's data on which it makes decisions.

Summary

Once data is integrated, the data becomes a foundation on which the corporation can make decisions and have confidence in those decisions. A foundation of integrated data allows the corporation to:

- Have confidence in the data on which decisions are made
- Allows the data to be accessed consistently
- Allows the data to be accessed quickly
- Allows anyone in the corporation access to the data

In a word, integrated corporate data forms the foundation for reliable decisions. A corporation can do meaningful business intelligence when it has integrated data. Stated differently, without an integrated foundation of data, an organization only has guesswork to guide decision-making.

Integrating data leads the organization to an interesting place. As long as data is unintegrated, the organization has to make decisions reactively. But once integrated data becomes available, organizations can operate proactively.

CHAPTER 2

Integrating Structured Data

The first place most people start noticing the need for data integration is structured data. Structured data is that data where the same structure of data repeats over and over. The content is different for each cell of data, but the structure is the same. Structured data includes records of banking transactions, sales, phone calls, etc.

Silos of data

Typically we store structured data in silos where one silo is defined and constructed differently from all other silos. It is challenging to analyze data coming from different silos. The silos of data are like different communities where there is no interaction from one silo to another. There are different ways in which siloed information needs to be analyzed and integrated, including:

- **Semantic integration**. The names that are attached to data
- **Calculations integration**. The way that data may be calculated or otherwise algorithmically treated

- **Selection integration.** The way data is selected for inclusion or exclusion from a project
- **Lineage integration.** The way that data is passed from one location to another

Semantic	Calculation	Selection	Lineage
Database	Formula	Inclusion	Source
Attribute	Summarization	Exclusion	Extraction
Keys		Timing	
Index			
Encoding			
Measurement			
Format			
Definition			
KPI			

Table 2-1. To create an enterprise view of the data, it is necessary to integrate the data within these silos of information. There are different ways to integrate structured data.

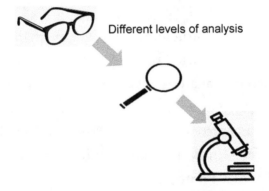

Different levels of analysis

Figure 2-1. Another way of considering the integration of siloed structured information is that some data needs one level of analysis, and other data needs a different level of analysis. For example, we can examine data with a pair of eyeglasses, a magnifying glass, or a microscope.

In some cases, multiple databases may have the same data which we can integrate. In other cases, it may be necessary to go to the attribute level and declare that two different attributes are the same or similar to integrate the data. In other cases, it may be necessary to look at the formula used to calculate data to integrate it. In other cases, it may be necessary to look at the selection criteria for data (inclusion or exclusion), or even data lineage, to integrate the data.

Types of integration

Different data requires different levels of explanation of how the data can be rationally merged or compared.

Database integration

In the simplest and highest level of analysis, it may be only necessary to say that two databases, such as Customer and Purchaser, have the same information. In this case, it is sufficient to say that database ABC has the same data as database BCD. The implication is that the databases are the equivalent of each other. Only infrequently is it sufficient to say that two databases are merely related. In almost every case, integration requires a much more detailed level of analysis than just a cursory scan of the data residing in the database.

Attribute integration

A much more normal level of analysis for integrating data is that of the activity of attribute analysis. In attribute analysis, different attributes from different databases are equivocated. If the data attributes are not exactly the same, they are adjusted.

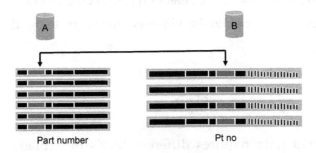

Part number   Pt no

Figure 2-2. As a simple example of integration at the attribute level, the analyst may say that Part number for database A is the same as Pt no in database B. In this case, only the names of the attributes of data are equivocated.

Key integration

Key integration is the same thing as attribute integration with one difference. In key integration, the key uniquely identifies the row it is in, whereas in attribute integration, the attribute identifies, but not uniquely, the row it is in. For example, a customer account number uniquely identifies the row in which it resides, but the state the customer lives in does not uniquely identify the customer. Many customers can live in the same state.

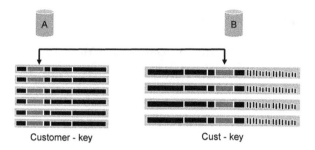

Figure 2-3. In A, Customer is key and in B, Cust is key. The keys are related. The relationship goes much further than the customers are related. Is the data found in one attribute compatible with data from the other database? Do they have the same encoding structure? The same format?

Index integration

Index integration is the same as attribute integration with one exception. That exception is that the attribute we need to integrate contains an index. Note that the index may be unique or not unique.

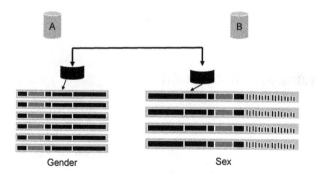

Figure 2-4. There is an index in database A on Gender and on Sex in database B.

Encoding integration

Encoding is the practice of assigning values to an attribute that has semantic meaning. As a simple example, in one database, gender is encoded as m/f and in another database, gender is encoded as male/female.

To integrate data, we need to harmonize the encoding schemes for each database. Stated differently, the data cannot be integrated operating under different encoding schemes.

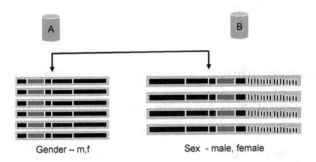

Figure 2-5. Gender is encoded one way in database A and another way in database B.

Measurement integration

To be compared, we must measure attributes the same way.

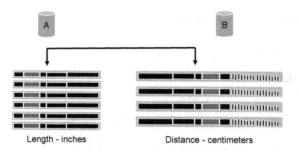

Length - inches   Distance - centimeters

Figure 2-6. Suppose the data in database A is measured in inches, and the data in database B is measured in feet. The data needs to be converted into a common measurement before we make a comparison.

Format integration

At a more detailed level of analysis, we can compare the physical characteristics of different attributes. It is necessary to have the physical definition of the data in a format that we can compare to other formats of data.

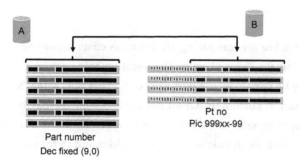

Pt no
Pic 999xx-99

Part number
Dec fixed (9,0)

Figure 2-7. The Part number in database A has a physical definition of dec fixed (9,0) and the attribute Pt no in database B has a format of Pic 999xx-99. To integrate this data, we need to resolve this format difference.

Definition integration

Perhaps the most important of all of the factors that go into integration is the factor of entity and attribute definition. Suppose we are comparing two different definitions of data. In that case, the comparison will be like comparing apples to oranges. Unfortunately, the actual definition of the data is often hard to discern. Understanding a given attribute's meaning usually takes a lot of digging. In the worst case, the analyst must return to the code handling the data and determine what logic was used to select and shape the data to understand its definition.

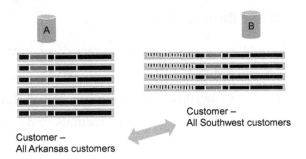

Customer –
All Southwest customers

Customer –
All Arkansas customers

Figure 2-8. We are comparing all Arkansas customers to all southwest
customers. Depending on the question being asked, the results
may be very biased. Southwest customers may actually include
Arkansas customers. Or all Arkansas customers may be for
people in Arkansas living in cities, and all southwest customers
may include people living in both cities and in the country.

The definitions need to be in alignment to make a meaningful comparison.

KPI integration

One of the important measurements of structured data is the measurement of Key Performance Indicators (KPIs). Typically KPIs are measured periodically, such as every week or month. To make a compelling comparison, the KPIs must be defined and calculated the same.

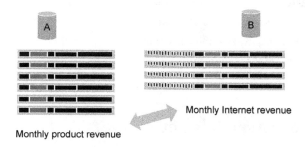

Monthly Internet revenue

Monthly product revenue

Figure 2-9. One KPI is for monthly product revenue and the other for monthly Internet revenue. These KPIs may sound the same but they measure very different things. Therefore, there cannot be a meaningful comparison of these values.

Calculations integration

We may calculate different attributes differently. When comparing the data, a comparison usually does not make sense unless the calculations align with each other.

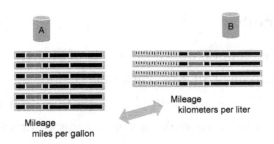

Figure 2-10. One measurement of mileage is calculated in miles per gallon, and another is calculated in kilometers per liter. Comparing the two measurements is folly unless a common measurement is determined.

Summarizations integration

We find summarizations in many places, including in calculating KPIs or common measurements. To compare summarizations, we need to ensure that the summarizations are created consistently.

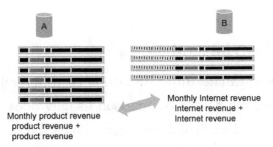

Figure 2-11. The data found in database A shows that the summarization is of product revenue. In database B, the summarization is for all the revenue generated over the Internet. Therefore, making a comparison between the two numbers can be a very difficult and misleading thing to do.

Selection criteria integration

Another factor that needs to be in alignment when comparing two values from different sources is data inclusion. For example, suppose one collection of data includes all data of one kind, and a similar collection of data from another source includes a different kind of data. In that case, comparing the two collections can be very questionable.

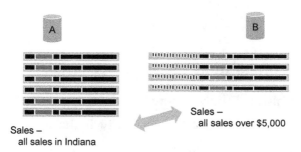

Figure 2-12. The data in database A is for all sales in Indiana. The data shown in database B is for all sales nationwide over $5,000. Comparing these two numbers will be very misleading.

Data exclusion integration

Since we've considered data we've included, we also need to consider data excluded from the calculation of a collection of data.

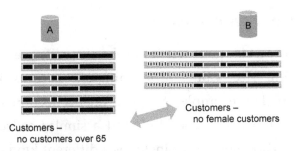

Figure 2-13. The data in database A excludes anyone younger than 65.
The data found in database B excludes all female customers.
Trying to compare the two can produce nonsensical results.

Lineage integration

We can also compare where the data has come from. The comparison may hold little validity if the data has come from very different sources.

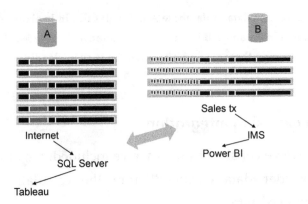

Figure 2-14. The data from database A has come from the Internet.
The data from database B has come from sales transactions.
Making a comparison may be an inappropriate thing to do.

Timing integration

In comparing data, we need to consider the moment of data collection. If two data collections have different timings, then the comparison of the data can become very misleading.

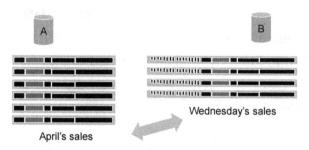

April's sales

Wednesday's sales

Figure 2-15. Database A has the sales for the month of April. Database B has the sales for Wednesday. Making a comparison of the two types of sales is nonsensical.

Transforming data

To make a meaningful comparison or combination of data coming from different sources of data requires that we take into consideration each of these types of integration. On occasion, we do not need to normalize the data to get a contrast in different kinds of data.

For example, comparing results obtained from the Internet with results obtained internally may be interesting. If that is the case, you don't want to normalize your data. But if you wish to add two types of data together and make a comparison, then we need to account for all types of integration. If you don't consider all these factors, you will add apples and oranges and get watermelons. And your watermelon will look strange.

Depending on what you want to do with the data, you can have different levels of transformation. In some cases, it is sufficient to know what data is related to other data. And in other cases, it is required that we fully and accurately harmonize the data.

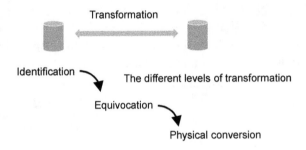

Figure 2-16. The level of integration depends entirely on three levels of analysis.

- Identification – what does the level of data represent
- Equivocation – what data is the same? What data is different
- Physical conversion – if we compare or add data, it must be physically converted into a common form. The common form it is converted into is the foundation of corporate data (or enterprise data).

Summary

Once data is placed into an enterprise format, the differences between the silos of data disappear.

It is easy to see why vendors and consultants are reluctant to tackle the task of integration. Addressing integration is a time-consuming, tedious, complex task where often guesses have to be made. In many cases, we cannot use documentation. In addition to the obvious factors, the truth is that many aspects of data are undocumented. Digging the considerations and conditions out of old source code is a difficult and ingratiating task. And that assumes that the old source code even exists, which sometimes is not true. And it assumes that the documentation is up to date, which it usually isn't.

Consider the Hubble space telescope as an example of what not to do. One engineer measured a part in inches, and another engineer measured a fitting part in centimeters. Unfortunately, the team discovered the error after launching Hubble and had to send a team into space to fix the problem and make the telescope usable. Moral of the story: get the conversions done properly and break down the silos.

CHAPTER 3

Integrating Textual Data

In addition to integrating structured data, an organization's decision-making process also requires the integration of text. There is more data wrapped up in text than there is in structured data.

Furthermore, great business value awaits the organization that starts to unlock the data in text. Text appears everywhere, including in emails, conversations, contracts, the Internet, and many other places.

The integration of text is very different from the integration of structured data. The closest commonality between the two integration processes is in the similarity between taxonomies and data models. From a high conceptual level, the data model is to the structured environment what taxonomies are to the textual environment.

Components of textual integration

Ingestion	Basic editing	Languages	Analytics
OCR	Proximity variables	English	Sentiment
Internet	Alternate spelling	Spanish	analysis
VTT	Stop word	Portuguese	Correlative
Email	Homographic resolution	French	analytics
Surveys	Stemming	German	Knowledge
	Taxonomic resolution	Italian	graphing
	Inline contextualization	Dutch	
	Document metadata	Arabic	
		Slang	
		Comments	
		Formal text	

Table 3-1. The components of textual integration.

Textual data architecture

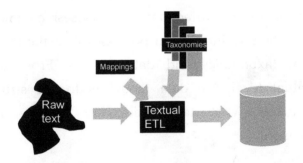

Figure 3-1. Raw text is ingested and read. Then, the raw text is passed to textual ETL and manipulated by textual mappings and taxonomical resolution. The result is a standard database. Once we create the standard database, analytical processing can ensue.

It is of note that the output of textual integration is the same output as the results of structured data integration. Text goes from being unstructured to being structured. A structured format allows analysis by standard analytical tools.

One significant difference exists between the different types of databases produced by integration. Context is static in the structured environment yet dynamic in the textual environment. In the case of structured data, the metadata provides the context in the form of static attribute names, table names, definitions, etc. The structured world has fixed attributes, definitions, and format records. On the other hand, in the textual world, context is dynamic. The user may be saying anything. It is up to textual ETL to recognize that context and dynamically incorporate it into the database created as part of textual integration.

Raw text can come in many forms from many places with idiosyncrasies:

- **Email**. The simplest form of text is the case where text is electronically available, such as in emails. Although emails are simple to process, they carry a large amount of overhead that is not of interest and often removed. In addition to extraneous system overhead, we also remove email spam and blather.

- **Voice**. We capture voice-born text on recordings, which are converted to electronic text using Voice to Text Transcription (VTT) technology. However, VTT technology is not 100% accurate in the transcription process.

- **Reports**. We use Optical Character Recognition (OCR) to convert printed reports into electronic text. As in the case of voice, some percentage of text on the paper will be transcripted incorrectly.

- **Internet**. Text on the Internet is usually in the form of electronic text. However, the data analyst using the Internet faces the obstacle of accessing text on the Internet. Many sites that display text on the Internet have arrangements to prevent the text from being lifted automatically. Furthermore, each Internet site is different. Therefore, if data is to be lifted off the Internet, there must be an individual scan process for each website accessed.

- **Spreadsheets**. There are several factors that the data analyst must be aware of in using text from spreadsheets. The first factor is that, under normal circumstances, numeric data cannot be lifted from a spreadsheet because numeric data has no reliable metadata that identifies the numeric data. For example, what does the number "7" mean? Standing by itself, the number "7" doesn't have meaning.

Preparing textual data for analytics

Deidentification of identifiers

Some text needs deidentification. Deidentification is taking a raw document and removing or encrypting data that identifies the document. Deidentification can take place for any data that will identify the person within the document. Data often deidentified includes:

- Name
- Social Security Number
- Telephone number
- Age
- Gender
- Date of birth

Deidentification occurs before the text ever leaves the confines of the organization owning and managing the text. Typical organizations that use deidentification include healthcare, military, and financial organizations.

Proximity analysis

When dealing with text, recognize that when two words appear near each other, they may have a special meaning.

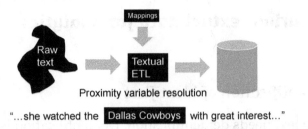

Figure 3-2. Suppose you encounter the words "Dallas Cowboys". When in proximity to each other, the Dallas Cowboys refers to a professional football team whose home is Dallas. But when those same words are separated, they mean something quite different. The word "Dallas" refers to a city in Texas and a "cowboy" is a person who rides a horse, tends cattle, and wears a Stetson hat.

Alternate spelling

Language has a generally accepted way in which words are spelled. However, on occasion, there are alternate ways to spell words.

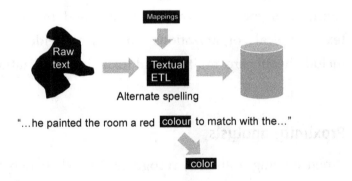

Figure 3-3. "Colour" is the British spelling of the word "color". The meaning is the same, but the spelling is different.

In addition to alternate spellings, the ability to recognize alternate spelling is quite useful in correcting misspellings. For example, the writer may write the word "judgement". The word "judgement" is properly spelled "judgment".

Another use of alternate spelling is recognizing that there are slang words and colloquialisms. For example, the writer may write the text – "ain't". "Ain't" is not a word but is a colloquialism for "isn't". Alternate spelling can interpret "ain't" to be "isn't".

Stop word resolution

Stop words are those words that are necessary for proper communication but are not central to the thought that is being communicated. Typical stop words are words such as "the", "a", "and", 'to", "which", and "that". To efficiently get at the nexus of what is being discussed in text, it is often useful to remove stop words.

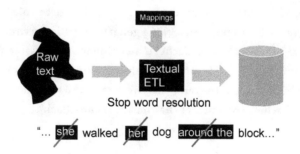

Figure 3-4. The stop words "she", "her", and "around the" are removed from text before further integration of the text occurs.

Homographic resolution

A homograph is a word that has more than one meaning. A homograph can be a word or an acronym. To properly interpret what is being said in text, it is sometimes necessary to use homographic resolution. In homographic resolution, we interpret the text by knowing who wrote the text. That is, the source of the text.

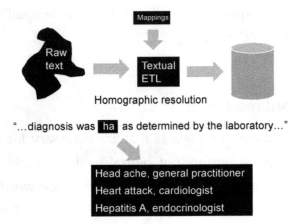

Figure 3-5. The term – "ha" – is encountered in reading doctor's notes. We determine the proper interpretation of "ha" by knowing the type of doctor who wrote the text. If a cardiologist wrote "ha", the reference is to a heart attack. If a general practitioner wrote "ha", the reference is to a headache. If an epidemiologist wrote "ha", the reference is to Hepatitis A. In interpreting homographs, it would be tragic if the term "ha" were read and was interpreted as "head ache" when in fact "ha" meant "heart attack".

Stemming

Stemming is the process of reducing a word to its Latin or Greek base. For example, the word "live" has several variations of the stem "liv". There are the words "lived", "living", "live", etc.

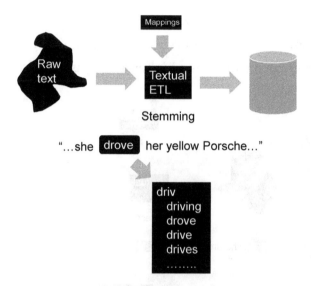

Figure 3-6. The word "drove" has a common stem of "driv". And "driv" has stems of "driving", "driven", etc.

Note that the stem itself may or may not be an actual word.

Taxonomical resolution

A taxonomy is a classification of words. A simple taxonomy might be:

- Trees
  - Elm
  - Cedar
  - Pecan
  - Mesquite

There are many taxonomies and types of taxonomies. Taxonomical resolution occurs when examining text and we recognize a word has a higher-level classification.

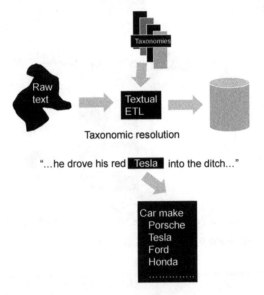

Figure 3-7. Tesla is recognized to be a make of car.

Taxonomies are an everyday part of speech. People use taxonomies regularly without even realizing that they are using taxonomies. A sentence as simple as "He drove his car" uses taxonomies. Car could refer to a Ford, Porsche, Hyundai, etc.

Inline contextualization

Most text is free form. No one tells you what to say when you have a phone conversation or when you write an email. As such, there is no predetermined pattern for text in most places where text appears. However, there are some places where text occurs in a predictable manner. For example, in a boiler plate contract, the lawyer creates a standard contract where the customer or merchant completes only a few lines.

Under these circumstances, text becomes predictable. When text becomes predictable, it is possible to use the technique of inline contextualization to identify and classify text.

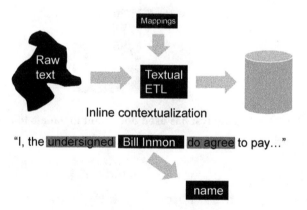

Figure 3-8. The name "Bill Inmon" is recognized by the appearance of a beginning delimiter and an ending delimiter. The beginning delimiter is the word "undersigned" and the ending delimiter are the words "do agree". The words between the delimiters are recognized to be a customer's name.

Classification

Sometimes instead of going into the document, we just need to classify the document. In almost every case, documents have some form of metadata attached to them. Different vendors have different forms of document-related metadata, such as document name, date, author, and so forth.

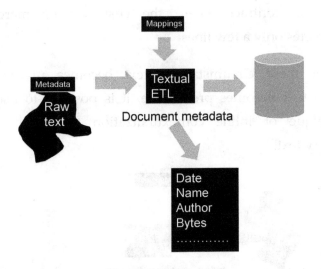

Figure 3-9. The data analyst has used document metadata to classify the document.

A collection of document metadata serves the same purpose as the library catalog in a library. We use the library catalog to quickly sort through many documents to find the document of interest.

Acronym resolution

Some professions, such as medicine, make liberal use of acronyms. When reading and transforming text, it is often necessary to resolve the acronyms to determine the meaning within the discussion.

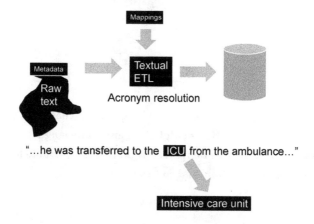

Figure 3-10. The term "ICU" is transformed into "intensive care unit".

Language awareness

All documents occur in some language:

- English
- Spanish
- Portuguese
- Arabic

To integrate text, the data analyst has to be aware of and account for the language(s) of the documents.

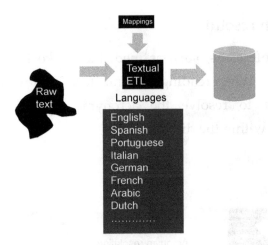

Figure 3-11. Reading and interpreting languages is challenging because there are different alphabets and some languages are very different such as being read right to left, bottom to top, having no punctuation, and so forth.

Text variations

Another factor that arises when integrating text is the fact that there are different types of text. There is formal text, such as what appears in a book. There is slang, including colloquialisms. There are comments which are often not complete sentences. There are laboratory reports where results are merely listed.

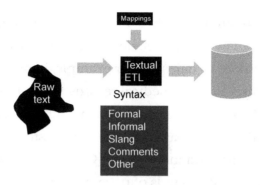

Figure 3-12. The data analyst needs to deal with various types of text during integration.

Performing analytics on textual data

There are all kinds of analytics that can be done with the databases that are created after textual integration. Now that text is in the form of a database, there is no limit to how many documents we can analyze. We can use techniques such as:

- **Sentiment analysis.** Sentiment analysis is the analysis of what a body of customers says about an organization or its products and services. Companies that wish to grow and thrive listen to their customers. Hearing the voice of your customer puts an organization in a proactive position in addressing the issues of customer retention and customer acceptance of the organization's products and services.

- **Correlative analytics.** In correlative analytics, we can analyze what relationships exist between variables or datasets. For example, in medicine, the analyst looks at medical records to determine what factors are associated with what other factors in studying a disease. For example, in studying the incidence and morbidity of COVID, an analyst can examine thousands of patients' medical records to determine the role of factors such as smoking, cancer, heart disease, diabetes, gender, and age.

- **Knowledge graphs.** One of the creative ways to display text is through the visualization technique known as knowledge graphing. In a knowledge graph, we identify the relationship and relationship strength between any two words or phrases. We can turn the text within a database produced from Textual ETL into a knowledge graph.

Summary

We have covered the similarities and differences of both structured and textual integration. For example, there is no inline contextualization in structured integration, just as there is no encoding resolution in textual integration. However, the result of integration is a structured database that allows the analyst to perform standard analytical processing.

CHAPTER 4

Mechanics of Integration

Although both structured data and textual integration result in the same kind of output, the steps to get there are very different. We need to adjust structured data during structured integration. However, we convert raw text to a structured database and recognize the text's context during textual integration.

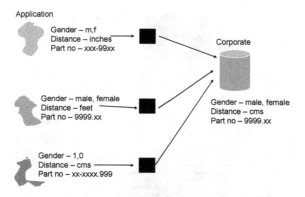

Figure 4-1. Structured data example. Although gender is encoded differently in each application, there must be one encoding scheme after integration. In this case, the first application has to have gender converted from m,f to male and female. In the third application, we convert from 1 and 0 to male and female. We must also convert distance and part number. In the final analysis, there is only one corporate definition and structure for data.

The final result of textual integration is a relational database with the text and the context identified. We complete two database phases for textual integration. The "phase one database" is the first step in understanding sentiment. In the phase one database, the important words are recognized and plucked out of the text. Then the context of those words is determined. This simple database makes the transition from text to a database.

My husband ordered the crab legs ($31.99) and it came with two sides. Most of the side dishes are a hefty extra charge $2.50 and up. What a scam. So he got the brussel sprouts (bland) and roasted potatoes (dry and flavorless).
I ordered the fish and chips and substituted the chips for mashed potatoes. In the many years I've been eating fish and chips, I have NEVER been served worse. ONE haddock filet battered and fried and plopped on the plate with a plop of mashed potatoes. No garnish. The plate looked pathetic. If I were the waitress, I'd be humiliated to serve a plate that looked like that. The filet was curled way up at the tail end and looked so weird. The fish was mealy and the batter was soggy - not crispy at all. The mashed potatoes were not good.

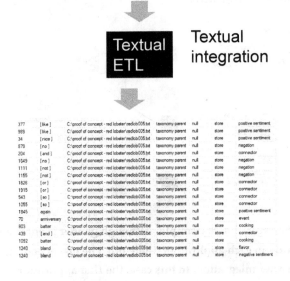

377	[like]	C:\proof of concept - red lobster\redlob005.txt	taxonomy parent	null	store	positive sentiment
989	[like]	C:\proof of concept - red lobster\redlob005.txt	taxonomy parent	null	store	positive sentiment
34	[nice]	C:\proof of concept - red lobster\redlob005.txt	taxonomy parent	null	store	positive sentiment
879	[no]	C:\proof of concept - red lobster\redlob005.txt	taxonomy parent	null	store	negation
204	[and]	C:\proof of concept - red lobster\redlob005.txt	taxonomy parent	null	store	connector
1649	[no]	C:\proof of concept - red lobster\redlob005.txt	taxonomy parent	null	store	negation
1111	[not]	C:\proof of concept - red lobster\redlob005.txt	taxonomy parent	null	store	negation
1155	[not]	C:\proof of concept - red lobster\redlob005.txt	taxonomy parent	null	store	negation
1826	[or]	C:\proof of concept - red lobster\redlob005.txt	taxonomy parent	null	store	connector
1915	[or]	C:\proof of concept - red lobster\redlob005.txt	taxonomy parent	null	store	connector
543	[so]	C:\proof of concept - red lobster\redlob005.txt	taxonomy parent	null	store	connector
1055	[so]	C:\proof of concept - red lobster\redlob005.txt	taxonomy parent	null	store	connector
1845	again	C:\proof of concept - red lobster\redlob005.txt	taxonomy parent	null	store	positive sentiment
70	anniversary	C:\proof of concept - red lobster\redlob005.txt	taxonomy parent	null	store	event
803	batter	C:\proof of concept - red lobster\redlob005.txt	taxonomy parent	null	store	cooking
439	[and]	C:\proof of concept - red lobster\redlob005.txt	taxonomy parent	null	store	connector
1092	batter	C:\proof of concept - red lobster\redlob005.txt	taxonomy parent	null	store	cooking
1240	bland	C:\proof of concept - red lobster\redlob005.txt	taxonomy parent	null	store	flavor
1240	bland	C:\proof of concept - red lobster\redlob005.txt	taxonomy parent	null	store	negative sentiment

Figure 4-2. Textual integration example phase one database. We enter raw tax through Textual ETL, load the proper parameters needed to interpret Textual ETL, and convert text into data. We read and then convert this text into a standard structured database.

However, to determine sentiment, we must perform a second level of analytics against the phase one database. In this phase two database, the analysis does such things as:

- Determining the scope of each sentence
- Recognizing and adjusting negation when negation occurs
- Finding the object of sentiment as well as the sentiment
- Determining the level of sentiment

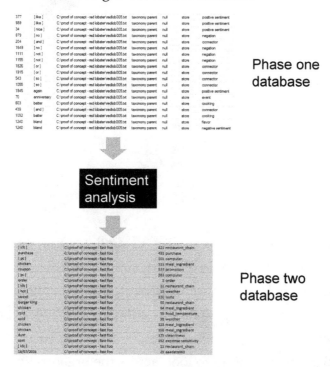

Figure 4-3. Textual integration example phase two database. Once we complete the second level of analytics, it is possible to use this database for analytical processing.

For both structured and textual data, our goal is a standard relational database to access the data for analysis.

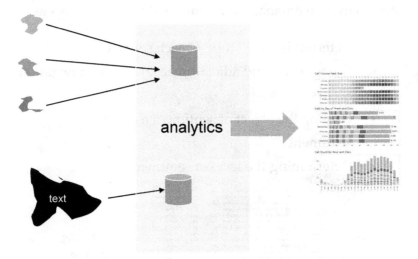

Figure 4-4. The organization can now look at enterprise-wide data and have confidence in the results.

Summary

As exciting as the possibility of finding and curating enterprise-wide data is and as simple as the database diagrams look, we must first overcome the integration obstacle. Integrating data is complex, tedious, time-consuming, and difficult. However, the product of all of this work is the ability to look across the organization and find an accurate assessment of data.

CHAPTER 5

Combining Structured and Textual Data

After integrating structured data and integrating textual data, can we combine them for further and more intensive analysis?

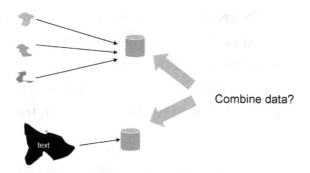

Figure 5-1. Unfortunately, the two types of data do not mix in many cases. So, forethought and analysis are required before we attempt to mix the different kinds of data.

We first need to determine if there is a good business reason for mixing the two data types. If there is little or no business value in mixing the data types, it is a waste of time to try to make a mixture happen.

An intersection of data

After confirming business value, determine whether there is some amount of intersection across the two different kinds of data. There are lots of reasons for the minimal or non-existence intersection of textual and structured data. The most basic reason is that the data found in the two environments is very different.

Structured data is typically transaction-based data where a transaction occurs, and we create a record of what has transpired. Textual data is quite different. Textual data occurs in a conversation or a written format. The person creating the text operates in a free-form fashion. In normal circumstances, the person does not talk in terms of keys and attributes. Instead, conversations take a natural and unpredictable flow, free of the jargon found in transaction processing.

There are, however, many circumstances where there is no logical or physical connection between the structured and textual data. In most circumstances, analyzing both kinds of data does not make business sense. As an example of no intersection in the data, consider the weekend scores of the NFL and a summary of the Easter egg hunt at the White House. It is far-fetched to think there is any relationship between these two types of data. These two events are simply unrelated. And accordingly, the integrated data generated from these two events is also unrelated.

An interior view

An exterior view

Key
    attribute
    attribute
    attribute
    attribute
    ....

Word
    byte address
    source
    context
    other
    ....

Figure 5-2. A convenient way of thinking about structured data and textual data is that structured data is an internal view of a corporation and textual data is an external view of the data. Structured data is data that portrays the finite interior of the corporation. Structured data looks at such things as bank deposits, purchases at the mall, and the recording of an airline reservation. Textual data looks at the words people use. Textual data can be about anything that is on a person's mind.

Restaurant example (low overlap)

Consider a restaurant as an example of a small overlap between textual data and structured data.

The restaurant has structured data, such as the records representing:

- The meals that have been served
- The price that people have paid
- The weekly revenue of the restaurant
- The number of diners on a day-by-day basis

Then there is the textual data found for the restaurant. Much of the textual data exists on the Internet, surveys, and elsewhere. The textual data contains the comments made by the customers of the restaurant. The types of things the customers talk about include:

- The food that was served
- The service of the waiter/waitress
- The price of the food
- The cleanliness of the restaurant
- And many other topics that relate to the experience of dining.

Common to both types of data are the restaurant name, store number, location, and so forth.

It is easy enough to collect feedback from the customers. Internet sites like Yelp contain places for people to express their feelings. Once the comments are gathered, the analyst passes them through Textual ETL, where they are gathered, read, and analyzed. Next, we produce a database that expresses customers' sentiment.

We create a structured database expressing the customer's feelings from these textual comments.

The negative comments are gathered together and are divided by store number. One store is for the restaurant in Boston, another in Dallas, and another in Atlanta. Next, the negative comments compilations are placed into a graph and matched with their applicable store. In creating this visualization, the stores with the most complaints start to show. Unfortunately, such a simple analysis can be very deceiving. For the analysis to be credible, it is necessary to factor in the revenue and the number of meals served for each store. This normalization of data is necessary because the mere raw ranking of complaints by store does not account for the fact that different stores have a vastly different number of customers. For example, if you were comparing a store in New York City with a store in Gallup, New Mexico, the store in New York will likely have a lot more complaints simply because there are many more customers in New York City.

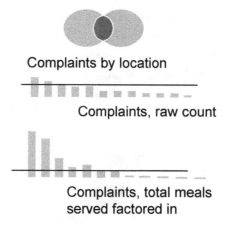

Figure 5-3. To have a valid tool for analytics, it is necessary to bring in structured data that can be used to factor in the number of customers served regularly. Once we combine structured and unstructured data, there is a real basis for analytics. Once we factor in the total number of meals a store serves, we have a much more accurate and realistic complaint picture.

As a related example of a small intersection between structured and textual data, consider the meals served and the Yelp ratings of this restaurant.

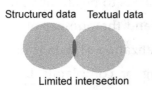

Structured data   Textual data

Limited intersection

Red Lobster, Ft Lauderdale	Yelp
July 13 – party of four $168.42	Rating – 1
July 13 – party of 2 $83.98	Restaurant – San Francisco
July 14 – Party of 6 $197.54	Dec 12
July 14 – party of 1 - $67.87	The biscuits were delicious. The crab was
July 14 – party of 3 - $105.87	A little undercooked. The mai tai was great.
....	We will be back.

Figure 5-4. There is a tally of the meals served by a restaurant and the Yelp rating. The structured data contains the number of people served, the date of the meal, and the total charge for the meal. The Yelp ratings contain the comments made by one of the customers about their meal. In addition, the structured and textual data contain the restaurant's location.

We can query the structured data to determine which restaurant served the most meals. The textual data can be queried looking at such things as:

- Menu items mentioned
- Service
- Restaurant ambiance
- Pricing

And an assessment of the feelings, positive or negative, of the items discussed.

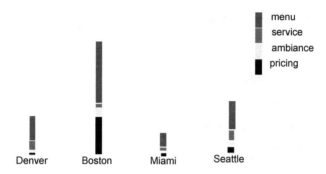

Figure 5-5. Once the data is collected, we can analyze each restaurant in the chain.

The analysis shows lots of interesting things. The analysis shows such things as:

- Which restaurants serve the most meals
- In which marketplace pricing is an issue
- In which marketplace there is an emphasis placed on menu items
- Where service is an issue

Analytics such as those shown can be very useful in managing a large chain of restaurants.

Airline example (high overlap)

As an example of an abundance of information overlapping the two environments, consider the information about airlines and what customers say about the airline. In this case, the customer gives very specific information about the flight date, airline, and route covered. If desired, the analytics could go into such details as:

- The pilots of the flight
- The food served
- The seating of passengers
- The length of the flight

The data that connects the two environments is quite strong. Of course, many of the details of the flight are extraneous. But if desired, the opportunity is there to strengthen the ties between the structured and textual worlds.

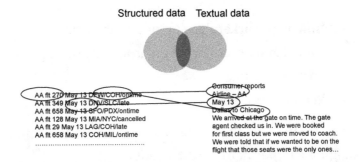

Figure 5-6. It is seen that there are multiple points of overlap of data.

There are then varying degrees of intersection between textual data and structured data. The degree to which it makes sense to try to relate the different kinds of data depends on:

- The business value to be made by intersecting the data

- The amount of interconnection of the data
- The business value to be derived by intersecting the data
- The amount of data that is available to be analyzed

Universal common connectors

In the case of no other connectors between the structured and textual environments, you can use "universal common connectors". Universal common connectors can always connect data, even when it does not make sense. There are three basic universal common connectors:

Regardless of the event and the conversation, there is always:

- A location the event or the conversation occurred at (Geography)
- A time the event or the conversation occurred at (Time)
- Some amount of money connected to the event or conversation (Money)

Money is not applicable in every case, but it is applicable often enough to be a universal common connector.

Car manufacturer and repair shop example (very low overlap)

The only commonality between a car manufacturer and repair shop is the make and year of the car. The car manufacturer has a lot of data about the manufacture of the car:

- Where it was made
- When it was made
- The color of the car
- The make of the car
- Where the car was shipped after manufacture

And so forth.

The repair shop has information such as:

- The make and year model of the car
- The nature of the accident
- The amount of damage that was sustained
- The location where the accident occurred

And so forth.

At first glance, very little information is common between the manufacturer and the repair shop. However, the location the car was shipped to and the location of the wreck or mishap might be useful pieces of information.

By focusing the information between the two data types on location, there may be some interesting conclusions. The conclusions that might be drawn:

- Cars in Montana and Colorado need extra attention paid to the manufacture and longevity of brakes because of the snow and mountains that the car is going to have to traverse
- Cars in Florida and Georgia need to have special attention to the underpinning of the car because of the exposure to salt water
- Cars in San Francisco need to have very reliable fog lights

One of the reasons for integrating text and structured data is the possibility of doing analytics on both at once.

Summary

There is a strong case for merging textual data with structured data if the merger makes business sense.

CHAPTER 6

A Project Plan for Integrating Structured Data

It is one thing to know the different integration components for structured systems. It is another thing to know the mechanics of integration. But how is a project organized to integrate structured data?

The starting point is to recognize what is happening. Most organizations start with silos of information that we cannot relate to each other. These silos grow over time. Trying to change an existing silo is a useless task. In almost every case, you will not be making major alterations to the silo itself. Or we make changes to the silo at a very slow pace.

Instead, the strategy is to access the data in the silo, integrate the data once released from the silo, and then build a pool of shared data, which represents the foundation of data for the corporation. In a sentence, that is the plan for releasing siloed data from its cage.

Step 1: Scope

How should you proceed when you start to integrate data from the silos of information that exist? When you try to attack all of your siloed information all at once, the usual result is a colossal failure. For many reasons, it makes sense to strategically attack your silos of information, one information system at a time.

A typical plan is to prioritize which systems should be attacked first, then second, and so forth. As long as your data model is a true enterprise data model, it is not a problem to take this approach. You break a massive problem into a series of smaller problems. And it is always easier to solve a series of smaller problems than to try to solve a single massive problem.

When you approach the problem of attacking the siloes of information a system at a time, you create an approach that, over time, moves data from the silo to the integrated pool of data. In doing so, you create a true enterprise view of data.

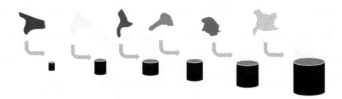

Figure 6-1. You create a stepladder of progress with each integrated database building on the previously built integrated database.

You can start to do analytics on the newly integrated pool of data as soon as you create the first iteration. There is no reason to wait until all data is added before starting analytical processing.

The speed of draining siloed data into the pool of integrated data depends on many factors, including:

- The volume of data
- The degree of complexity that the integration of data entails
- The availability of resources to work on the integration of data
- The criticality of the data

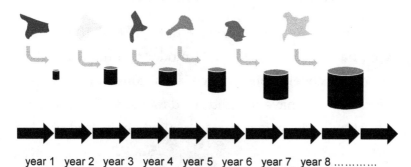

year 1   year 2   year 3   year 4   year 5   year 6   year 7   year 8 ....

Figure 6-2. A typical plan for integrating data from the siloed environment to the integrated pool of data may take years. It is unlikely that such a plan would take months, although it is possible. Integrating structured data is a long-term project. It just does not happen overnight.

Step 2: Model

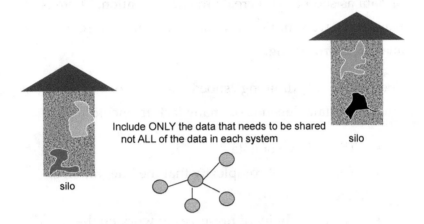

Figure 6-3. The first step in releasing the siloed data from its cage is to model what the output data needs to look like. The output data is the data that will reside in the shared pool of data.

You can usually purchase the data model. If possible, avoid having to build the data model you need. Building the data model from scratch is a long and complex exercise. If you have to build the data model from scratch, at least build the data model incrementally instead of all at once.

If you do have to build your own data models, recognize that the only data that belongs in the model is that data that needs to be shared within the organization. Trying to model every scrap of data in the organization is a waste of resources.

Step 3: Map

Once you have the model in a usable state, you can then use the model for mapping the siloed application data into the pool of commonly shared data. The mapping of the data looks at the siloed application data and determines what the data needs to have done to it before becoming corporate data.

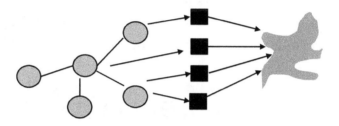

Figure 6-4. Create a mapping from the data model to an application.

Maintain this mapping in a corporate directory, which serves both as a guideline for future development efforts and as a documentation of the thinking when the mapping was created. In addition, the corporate directory needs to be updated periodically as the mapping changes and as new data is added or modified.

The mapping and placement of the mapping into the corporate directory are constantly being added to as we add more applications. That is, the mapping process is an ongoing task.

Step 4: Create a central pool of shared data

The model and mapping are used to create the transformation logic. Usually, the transformation logic is automated with ETL technology. Of course, we can always manually perform ETL. But it is usually much more efficient to use an automated tool such as ETL technology to take the mapping logic and transform it into code. The process of loading data into the central pool of shared data takes place over time. First, we create one part of the pool. Then another, and so forth. Trying to create the pool all at once is a serious mistake.

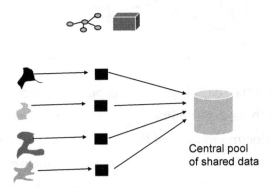

Central pool
of shared data

Figure 6-5. Use the model and mapping to create a central pool of shared data.

Advantages of the plan

The project plan for integrating structured data from a silo has many advantages:

- **Incremental changes**. One of the major advantages is that the data model, the mapping, and the directory can all be changed incrementally over time. In the same vein, building the common pool of shared data is an ongoing activity. The infrastructure is such that we can easily make adjustments over time with no disruption to existing systems. There are no code rewrites or alterations to existing databases, and the siloed environment can be left in peace with no disruptions. The only requirement is that the siloed applications have to allow access to the data in the silo. Other than that, the siloed systems are not in the least bit affected by the building of corporate data.

- **Backward referencibility**. We design the data to be referenced in a backward manner. If there is ever any doubt as to the origin of data or the transformation processes built into the architecture, the data at any point can be referenced back to its source.

- **Choice of data**. This plan makes it easy to get either siloed data or enterprise data, whichever you wish. If someone wishes to look at siloed data they can. If someone wishes to look at enterprise data they can.

- **Resolution**. If there happens to occur a discrepancy or anomaly in the data or mapping process, the simple architecture that has been described makes it easy to find and resolve the discrepancy.

Summary

Because the architecture does not disrupt siloed data, there are minimal political discussions about the inclusion of enterprise data along with siloed data. And if there are any disputes as to the accuracy of or validity to the data, the mapping allows the discussions to have a base of reality.

With the many advantages of having an incremental, non-disruptive plan for migrating away from the siloed environment, the siloed environment slowly shrinks. Once people find out there is vetted, curated, reliable corporate data, there is less and less reliance on siloed data.

.

CHAPTER 7

A Project Plan for Integrating Textual Data

In some ways, integrating textual data is more straightforward than integrating siloed structured data. That is because there are tools designed specifically for the task. On the other hand, language is very complex. One of the features of language is that it is imprecise. Unlike much processing in the structured environment, there are no definite answers in the textual environment. Instead, there are statistically significant answers.

In the world of text, perfectionism is an enemy, not a friend.

Step 1: Select the scope

The first step in deciding how to proceed in textual integration is to determine your general scope. For example, you might select auto manufacturing, cardiovascular medicine, or retail sales over the Internet.

The selection of scope sets the stage for the understanding of context.

There are different ways of processing text. For example, text from medicine will be processed differently from text from law which will be processed differently than text from engineering, and so forth.

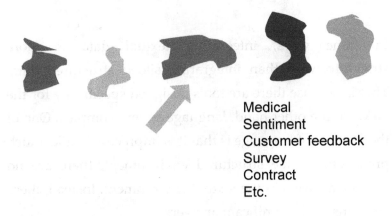

Medical
Sentiment
Customer feedback
Survey
Contract
Etc.

Figure 7-1. The first step is to define the scope of what type of text you want to integrate.

The first question to be asked when deciding to integrate text is, "Where do we start?" We start where there is the biggest impact on our business. That is, with the areas of your organization that will benefit the most by analyzing text. To find out the best place to start, answer questions such as:

- What is critical to the business?
- What text is accessible?
- What text is finite in scope?

Step 2: Find ontologies/taxonomies

The second step is to select, or otherwise acquire, the taxonomies/ontologies you will use to process the text you want to integrate.

There are many ways to acquire a taxonomy. One way is to build it yourself. Most organizations do not have the skill set to build a taxonomy. Another approach is to acquire a commercially available taxonomy. Some organizations have taxonomies for sale. It is an easy and inexpensive way to acquire a commercial taxonomy. Of course, every commercially developed taxonomy requires a certain amount of customization once acquired. But it is much easier to customize an existing taxonomy than to create one from scratch. A third possibility is to use one or more of the taxonomies available through the purveyor of Textual ETL.

For example, suppose you have chosen the world of medicine as your scope of integration. And suppose you have chosen diabetes and cardiovascular as the type of text you want to integrate. You would not select a taxonomy for accounting, engineering, or education. Instead, you would choose taxonomies/ontologies specific to diabetes and cardiovascular medicine as the basis for your processing.

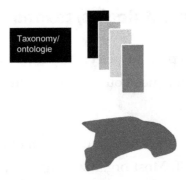

Figure 7-2. Next either develop taxonomies or use existing taxonomies or develop other mappings.

Step 3: Load the taxonomies

The next step is to load the taxonomies into the Textual ETL processor. After you have loaded the taxonomies/ontologies into Textual ETL, you can ingest the raw text for processing. Unless there is a conversion or reformatting of the taxonomy, this process takes only a minute or two.

Step 4: Ingest raw text

After loading the taxonomies, you tee up the text to be analyzed and let Textual ETL do its own processing. Depending on the amount of data you want to process, this may take a few minutes to a few hours. When Textual ETL is finished processing, the raw databases are ready.

The ingestion of raw text may be easy or difficult. Use VTT technology if your data is on a voice recording, OCR for printed text, or download the text from the Internet.

If your text is already in an accessible electronic format, you can just use it directly.

Textual ETL reads your text and processes it. The output from Textual ETL is a standard database with several features:

- The word or phrase that in the raw text is captured
- The context of the word is disclosed
- The location of the word in the originating document

The database also captures sentence punctuation, negation, degree of sentiment, and so forth. You can then take the database and start to do analytics against it. Depending on the analytics you want, you may have to do a second step of database processing.

Step 5: Determining analytical processes

The next step is to determine what kind of analytical processing you want to support. Do you want to support sentiment analysis? Do you want to support correlative analysis? Do you want to support basket analysis? Do you want to support other kinds of analysis?

How you do the extraction and processing of text set the stage for the kind of analysis you want to do.

If you want to do sentiment analysis, you need to take the database that has been captured and do a second-level analysis on top of it. The second level analysis looks at each sentence and determines if there is sentiment to be found in the sentence. In addition, the second level analysis looks for the negation of sentiment to determine if the sentiment has been negated, such as, "I did not like the enchilada."

Another kind of secondary analytics is correlative analytics. In correlative analytics, you find the correlation between words and concepts. For example, suppose you have the medical records of 10,000 patients who have had COVID. In that case, you can find out from the patient the correlating factors to COVID, such as smoking, cancer, diabetes, or obesity.

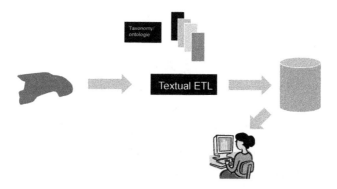

Figure 7-3. Once you have the data in the form of a database, you can use any standard analytical tool you want to do whatever analytics you want.

So how long does the process of integrating text take? Of course, the length of time depends on the particulars of your text that you want to process and the type of analytics you want to do. Some of the factors that affect how long the textual integration process will take are:

- The volume of text you have to process
- The complexity of the text to be processed
- The availability of an appropriate taxonomy/ontology
- Whether or not this is your first time running this type of text through Textual ETL
- The type of analytics you wish to do

And as soon as the first data is available, analysis can commence. Of course, the greater the amount of data, the more robust and the more sophisticated the analysis can be.

An iterative process

Building the textually integrated database is iterative. First, we add one type of data, then another, and so forth.

One of the essential ingredients is the data model and/or the ontologies used to process the raw text. There are several places where the taxonomy/ontology can come from.

One of those places is the raw text itself. It is fairly simple to read the raw text and then derive the raw data into the textual taxonomy. An alternative is to find the taxonomy you wish to have from the Internet. In almost every case, we must customize the Internet-based taxonomy prior to use. A third possibility is selecting a taxonomy from a commercially available source. Organizations such as Wand, Inc have various commercially available taxonomies. And finally, there is always the possibility of reusing a taxonomy that you might have. And, of course, there is nothing to say that you can't take a taxonomy from more than one source.

Summary

Initially, building a database from text seems overwhelming. And without the right tools, it is indeed an overwhelming task. But given the right tools, building a database to do analytical processing based on text is fast and easy. The task seems to be quite simple if you know what you are doing.

Can the two different types of integration – structured data and textual integration be done in parallel? Of course! The only limiting factor is the manpower dedicated to both projects. However, textual integration occurs at a much greater speed than structured integration. Results from textual integration occur in terms of days and weeks. Output from structural integration occurs in terms of quarters and years. In other words, textual integration is a jackrabbit, and structured text integration is a tortoise.

CHAPTER 8

Integration Best Practices

Data integration can be simply described as merging data into one environment. This can become more complex by adding merged data from multiple systems or sources, and normalizing it so it correctly represents the same type data from multiple systems in one environment. It can include standardizing data so similar types of data look and react in the same manner. It can include internal data where internal standards may have been applied to the data structures helping with the task of data merging. It can also include external data where data may have quality issues and requires additional effort to make it consistent with the other data sets. It can include structured data where databases have a required structure or unstructured data, such as text, where data can have multiple meanings and be interpreted in different ways. It can be physically brought together into one physical data structure, or it can be distributed across many structures or remain in place.

The purpose is to improve business strategies and decisions based on analyzing and evaluating data from different systems acting as distributed data silos. For example, we may bring together data from an organization's customers, products, ordering, sales, buyers, inventory, delivery, and distribution systems. It may include textual data from organization notes, customer surveys, and comments retrieved from the organization's website. It may include data from the Internet of Things (IoT) devices and sensors. It may include data provided by government or external organizations, including demographics and buying patterns of a community.

In some organizations, this has been a simple process of dumping data from each system into another environment, often in the cloud, and providing access to this new environment to their data analysts and data scientists.

One result of this type of integration is that the users spend more time identifying how to make sense of this data after finally finding what they believe they need. These users then must complete the "steps of integration" to ensure they are using the data correctly. And now, the definition of correct data belongs to each user with their knowledge about each specific dataset they use and analyze. As data continues to grow at an even faster pace, and more and more data is being dumped into this one environment, finding valuable pieces of data takes even longer and is more challenging.

Aim for true data integration

Some organizations take the extra step to truly integrate their structured and textual data from different systems into one environment by standardizing the data, so each piece of data has one name, one definition, one set of domain values, and one way for the users to access and understand the data. This type of integration requires implementing standards and data governance. A true integration of data in the integrated environment provides greater value than just bringing data together from disparate systems into one environment.

Although data integration is the most challenging and time-consuming task, it also provides the most value to the users and to the data-driven decisions and strategies they define from using this data.

Identify the fans of data integration

Data scientists and data analysts lead the charge for data integration because they need this data and need it to be linked together accurately. If the data is only available without integration, these users must complete data integration while accessing the data. First, they need to understand the formats, rules, taxonomy, domain values, quality rules, and definitions of each set of data. Then they need to establish a mapping of data from one set of data to another set by applying transformation rules so that data will equate to each other to make that data useful. Finally, they need to understand all sets of data that are part of the new integrated environment so the rules they apply accurately reflect integrated data.

End-users such as executives, managers, product designers, and sales and marketing managers also need integrated data. They need the direction and ideas of the data scientists and data analysts based on accurate data in their integrated environment.

Determine the data integration roles

Integrating data requires numerous skills and knowledge:

- **Business experts**. Business experts with product, service, and organizational knowledge are important for data integration. They know from a business perspective what the data means, its use, and how it relates to other data. They can help determine how to map one piece of data from one system to a piece of data from another system. They know and understand the taxonomy of their business, helping to sort through the challenges of adding textual data (such as design notes, customer comments concerning product experience, and surveys) into the integrated environment.

- **Application support team members**. These team members know and understand how the data is stored and retrieved. They know the data format, how to join data using tables and columns within the database structure, and what issues were resolved to ensure source data quality. In general, they know the history of this data. These team members are key to extracting and tying data together correctly from the source systems and mapping data together with pieces of data from other source systems.

- **Information or data governance team members**. These members work with data owners to help define each piece of data used within this integrated environment. Definitions consist of more than a simple definition in business terms, but also clear examples with valid domain values used to validate the data migrating into the integrated environment. They define the rules used for transformation and data that are critical or under classifications requiring different security levels. These team members ensure a data catalog and glossary are built and maintained, providing documentation of business names, business definitions with examples, transformation and data quality rules, domain values, and data classifications.

- **Analysts**. Analysts help develop the mapping documents to map each piece of data to pieces from other sources. This includes the transformation rules needed to transform each piece of data, along with domain values and data quality rules needed to ensure accurate data transformation.

- **ETL (Extract Transform and Load) and ELT developers**. These developers utilize the rules and mapping defined in the mapping documents to code the ETL and ELT processes. These processes migrate data from the source systems and external sources to the integrated environment. They ensure the correct transformations exist for each piece of data to be migrated, along with using the data quality rules and domain values to edit and validate the data. Many organizations establish standards for types of transformations that should occur at each hop of data migration from one to source to a target.

- **Test team members**. These members test the newly developed code to ensure the code meets all requirements defined in the mapping document. Migrated data also needs to be validated for accuracy based on the mapping document's domain values and data quality rules. These testers are needed when the integrated environment is ready for validation and data from multiple source systems can be evaluated and validated in the new integrated environment.

- **Integrated data end-users**. End-users consist of executives and managers who need information about their products and services. These end-users need to be open to using integrated data that provides perspectives that may differ from typical ideas and views. They may need to be able to think outside the box when queries or analytics produce a surprising result set. With integrated data, the tools might direct the organization down a path never traveled before.

- **Users**. Users include analytical team members, such as data analysts, data scientists, and statisticians. They understand the organization and taxonomy well enough to see patterns in data that the tools highlight. They need to understand the data using the definitions provided by information governance to understand better what the data tells them about their organization, products, and services. Data analysts and data scientists are common within major league sports. They use integrated environments with their analytics toolset to make decisions about plays, lineups, positioning players on the field with the "infield shift", trading specific players, or bringing in a new coaching staff. The more integrated data they can use from all areas of the professional sport, community, team, and culture, the greater help to management in running their business. Integrated data is at the center of this revolution in professional sports.

Stress the benefits of data integration

It is helpful for users and end-users of data-driven decisions to understand the challenges of integrating data and the value of accessing integrated data. Benefits include:

- **Data quality**. Users will see how data quality and integrity improve in the integrated environment and how data issues are identified and resolved in source applications. Statistics and measurements can be generated during the transformation processes to compare the source data to the domain values provided in the mapping documents and report matches and mismatches. Mismatches can be sent back to the source applications to help resolve and improve data in the source applications. Reporting data can also be provided by applying the data quality rules documented in the mapping documents to the source data. Data quality statistics can show improvements over time as the poor quality data is corrected in the source applications. Reporting data can also be provided for missing or outdated data by using rules for these issues in the transformation processes.

- **Collaboration**. A unified view of data across the entire organization provides an environment where it is easier for departments within an organization to collaborate and increase employee efficiency. Users will not waste time hunting down data and learning how to match to another set of data or combine this data with data from another department. Instead, the data is already available for users' analysis and evaluation in the integrated environment. Analysts can spend more time analyzing and determining what the data is saying.

- **Cross-training**. An integrated environment can also help provide cross-training and knowledge sharing across the organization. With distributed siloed applications, team members may not understand other departments and how these departments' work combines with theirs for the organization's success. With the integrated environment, they can learn about other departments and how their goals and purpose impact the health of their department and the entire organization.

- **Data analytics**. Data analytics is a process where programming techniques and statistical methods are combined to study the data and derive insights. Data analytics relies on algorithms and quantitative analysis to determine the relationship between data not clearly defined on the data model. Data analytics involves discovering, interpreting, and communicating meaningful patterns in data. The more accurate the data used by these tools, the better and more accurate the result sets will be.

Deploy a reusable process for new sources

For the integrated environment to remain a valuable asset to the organization, it needs to be managed and augmented with the periodic addition of new sources and data types. Business Subject Matter Experts (SMEs) and analysts must continually look for new data sources that can add value. We can reuse the initial set of standards, rules, and processes for data integration on a smaller scale for each new data set needed integrated with the existing integrated environment.

Many organizations will standardize on one source and relate all other data to this "standard" source of data. This approach sets the stage for adding new data sets to the integrated environment by comparing the new data set with this "standard" set. This approach improves the time to integrate new data sets since the "standard" set will be documented and understood by the implementation team. Processes developed to integrate other data sets will be continually used for these new data sets required for integration.

Update data often

A key to keeping the data meaningful in the integrated environment is to keep the data fresh and updated as often as updates are available in the source applications or from external sources. Data loses meaning quickly and becomes stale in today's ever-changing world. Making decisions with stale data can be worse than making decisions without any information.

For example, professional sports teams use integrated data with analytics to evaluate what and how to run the team as a business and plan the game with as much insight as can be found within the historical data from past games played. And the more current data from these teams will provide the best analytics and decisions, since players have their ups and downs and fresh data is required to identify how the team and its players are currently doing.

Define milestones

Milestones are specific points within an environment's life cycle used to measure the progress toward the ultimate goal. Milestones are created as gates for the building and use of the integrated environment. As a result, management can see the progress of building the integrated environment and its usage. Milestones include:

- Schedule for the rollout of different source data with the availability of different data sets. This could include a roadmap of different sources and sets of users to the new environment. It can include a rollout schedule for types of data (structured or textual).

- Specific deliverables of additional services (along with the source data), including monitoring, statistics, reporting, quality, and completeness checks. Reporting can include summary and detailed statistics, with numbers of data sources, data fields, quality fields, data integrity fields, and fields with quality or completeness issues.

- Retention of data along with purging and cleaning out of older data that should no longer be stored and used in the integrated environment.

- External reviews by end-users who have accountability for this data and the quality of this data.

- Budget reviews for information governance and data stewards responsible for this application, along with access to, use of, and reporting for this integrated environment.

Summary

Even though data integration has been performed for years and implemented with many different tools, it is still an evolving discipline because of the available approaches and techniques. There isn't a "one size fits all". Organizations' cultures, source applications, physical location of source data, source data structures, data governance maturity, key skillsets required, requirements for a compliant organization, and commitment of team members to build and use the integrated environment are all crucial factors.

With the increasing use of technology in business, organizations that recognize integrated data as an important asset will emerge at the top of their industry.

CHAPTER 9

Taxonomies and the Data Model

Taxonomies and data models are at the heart of integration. The data model is at the heart of integrating structured data. Taxonomies are at the heart of integrating text.

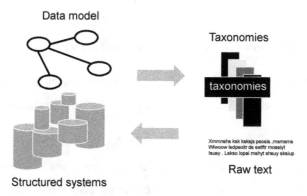

Figure 9-1. A natural question arises – are the data model and the taxonomy the same thing? The answer is no – there are distinct differences between the data model and the taxonomy.

Whenever the subject of taxonomies arises, it is normal for the reader to bring in the subject of ontologies. For many reasons, taxonomies and ontologies are closely intertwined.

Taxonomies and ontologies

So what does the relationship between an ontology and a taxonomy look like?

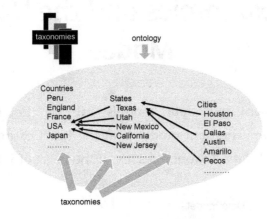

Figure 9-2. An ontology is a collection of related taxonomies.

There are other more academic definitions of an ontology, but for our discussion, we will use this simple definition.

In the example shown, the ontology is a description of geography. Geography contains countries, states, and cities. Each state relates to a country and each city relates to a state. There are multiple taxonomies within the ontology and there are relationships between the different taxonomies. As an example of an ontology, consider medicine to be an ontology. Within the medicine ontology, taxonomies include:

- Medications/drugs
- Procedures

- Symptoms
- Past medical history
- Social history

There are similar ontologies for accounting, law, education, manufacturing, and other industries.

In this chapter, we will reference taxonomies. But know that we can combine taxonomies into ontologies.

The purpose of data models and taxonomies

The data model and the taxonomy serve as high-level roadmaps for integrating structured data and text. When doing integration, it is easy to get lost in the details of the activities. The high-level road map provides clarity.

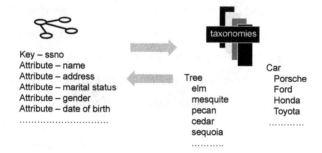

Figure 9-3. The data model and taxonomy also both have data and data structures embedded in their fiber. The data model has keys, attributes, and other data definitions. The taxonomy has classifications and the text we classify as part of the taxonomy.

Data model and taxonomy differences

There are two important differences between the data model and taxonomy:

- **Internal facing/external facing**. The data model is internal facing and the taxonomy is external facing. The data model depicts activities and objects internal to the corporation. The data model looks at products, customers, manufacturing processes, sales, and other items of interest to the corporation. The taxonomy, on the other hand, looks at the external world. The taxonomy looks at people, events, and objects outside the corporation. The taxonomy might be for products, companies, countries, or organizations outside the corporation.

- **Data mutability**. Another fundamental difference is understanding what can be done to the data. In a data model, you can always change the data if we need to correct something. With the taxonomy, you operate under a completely different set of assumptions. You cannot change text. It may even be illegal to change text, even if you wanted to make changes.

Summary

Both the data model and the taxonomy are important for integration. The data model and the taxonomy provide a frame of reference for integration. And integration is a long-term effort that requires long-term guidance.

Here is a summary of the similarities and differences:

	Data model	Taxonomy
Similar	Road map	
	Detailed data	
Difference	Internal	External
	Can be altered	Data cannot be altered

CHAPTER 10

Data Science and Integration

There is a symbiotic and important relationship between data science and integrated data. The foundation of data science is data. Without useful, reliable data, the data scientist cannot produce any meaningful and believable analysis. But with integrated, believable data, the data scientist can produce sophisticated analytics.

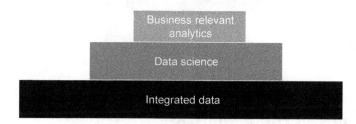

Figure 10-1. The foundation for data science is integrated data.

One of the challenges facing the organization is the data scientist who thinks they don't need the assistance of the data architect. Many data scientists graduate college with a good grasp of how to do statistical analytics only to find that when they get into the real world, they spend the vast majority of their time struggling with data. If the data scientist were operating on integrated, believable data, the scientist would be able to use the skills of a data scientist.

As long as the data scientist is operating on inaccessible, unintegrated data, the data scientist must spend huge amounts of time trying to make the data believable in the first place. The world that the data scientist faces when dealing with unintegrated, siloed-based data is one where no data is reliable. Also, it is difficult to access the data, find the meaning of the data, and relate the different attributes. For this reason, enterprise-wide integrated data is the data scientist's best friend.

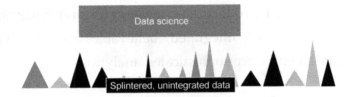

Figure 10-2. A foundation of unintegrated data.

Levels of commonality

There are three different types of commonality that exist within structured and textual data: technical, logical, and structural. In technical commonality, the different types of data exist in the same type of commonality. In logical commonality, there is some degree of commonality to the data. In structural commonality, the basic structure of the data is similar or identical. To do analytical processing, there needs to be some degree of commonality at some level of commonality among the types of data.

Technical commonality

An example of technical commonality is transforming text into a standard database format. Text is passed into Textual ETL where the text goes from raw text into a standard database where we can compare it to structured data.

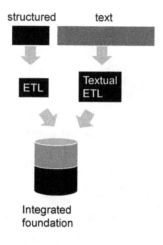

Figure 10-3. We can combine structured data and textual data.

Just because we can transform into a common technology does not necessarily mean we can perform data analysis. After we unify text in technology, there remains the problem of finding logical commonality of the data.

However, placing data in a common technological format is only the first step in allowing the data scientist to start to do analytics. There is much more to finding commonality of data than merely placing the data into the same technological foundation.

Analog/IoT data

If we can reduce structured data and text to a common technology, what about analog/IoT data?

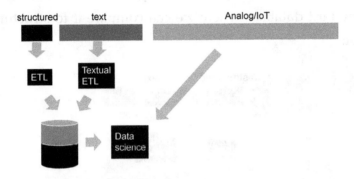

Figure 10-4. But what about analog/IoT data?

Analog/IoT data has a very different structure than structured or textual data. The differences between analog/IoT data and structured and textual data are such that trying to transform data into a common technical format is very difficult. It is therefore wise to apply separate forms of data science on the data.

Summary

Enterprise-wide integrated data forms the foundation that the data scientist needs to find the secrets and patterns in the data.

CHAPTER 11

Documentation and Integration

While data integration is the foundation of much analytic processing, integration is made much more useful if we enhance the integration process with documentation. Stated differently, proper documentation of the integration greatly accelerates this value and the efficacy of integration.

The documentation issue starts with examining who needs to know about the integration of data. Three audiences need to know how the organization has integrated data:

- **Developer**. The first audience needing to know about integration is the developer, who has to work daily with code and data. A developer not seeing what logic surrounds the data they are working on is like a pilot flying without eyesight. Disasters are lurking around every corner.

- **Analyst**. To do accurate and intelligent analysis, the analyst needs to know what data is in the system, where it came from, what it means, and how it has been calculated. Once the analyst knows these facts, doing an effective analysis becomes possible.

- **Database administrator (DBA).** The database administrator needs to know how data is structured and where the data comes from to do a good job of keeping the database alive and thriving.

Documentation components

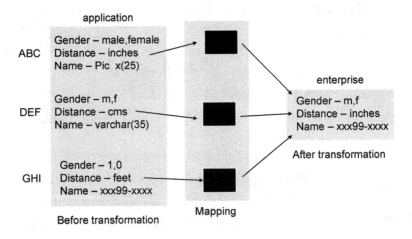

Figure 11-1. Metadata before and after transformation. The metadata before transformation includes the encoding for gender, the measurement of distance, and the physical embodiment of name. The mapping shows that gender is converted to m,f, distance is measured in inches, and the physical specification of name is xxx99-xxxx.

Documentation on data integration must consist of:

- The metadata before integration occurs
- The mapping of the integration itself (data lineage)
- The metadata of the data after integration occurs

The integration of text is a little bit different. There is no before metadata for text. We simply store the raw text as raw text.

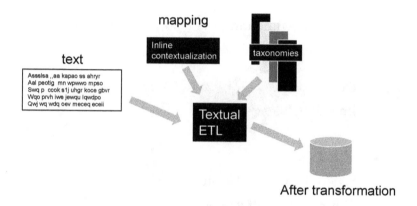

Figure 11-2. The transformation of the raw text is found in the inline contextualization mappings and in the taxonomies applied to the text. The output metadata appears in the metadata for the output file. Note that we can bury the data relationships inside the transformed database structure.

One of the most important components of documentation is the data lineage. The lineage needs to start from where the data enters the system and extends to the endpoint in the system. It is normal for data to flow through multiple states in its lifetime. The documentation of the data lineage should show the data's state, the transformation patterns, and the mapping of the transformations at each step of the way.

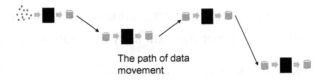

The path of data movement

Figure 11-3. The analyst should be able to use the lineage to trace the data from its origin to its final resting point.

In addition to documenting the before and after metadata states and lineage, we can also include:

- Definitions
- Encoding
- Profile
- Volumes
- Schedule of refreshment
- Normal range of values
- Historical track of structural changes

Summary

All people and applications needing to see the corporate integration data should have it immediately available. And of course, we need to keep documentation up to date. Having documentation that is not up to date is misleading and, in some ways, worse than having no documentation.

CHAPTER **12**

An Example of Integration

There are many moving parts to achieving integration across structured and textual data. Let's look at an example of all those parts in action. The following approach is but one of many possibilities for integrating data.

A merger

Suppose an organization wishes to merge two different branches, one in the United States and the other in Australia. Over the years, each branch has independently developed its own systems. These independent systems have been operating for years.

One day management decided to consolidate the customer information coming from these systems. While the two systems had similarities, it was challenging to create a consolidated analytical infrastructure based on very different treatments of data.

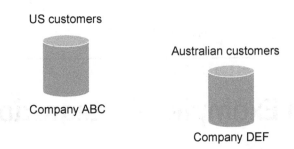

Figure 12-1. Management decided to start by integrating the two systems that capture customer information.

The organization appointed an integration team consisting of members from the US and Australia. Management decided that there needed to be people of different backgrounds that understood the data. There was scant documentation of the systems. Most of the knowledge of the systems was in the heads of the design committee participants.

The idea was to create a comprehensive database of the organization's customers. Complicating matters was the fact that there was overlap between the two databases. For various reasons, a small percentage of the customers existed in both databases.

For example, some people regularly travel between the US and Australia, others have immigrated to one or the other country, and a few people buy products from both branches randomly. But most customers were residents of one country, resulting in a manageable overlap between the two databases.

Challenges

There were many challenges to the merging of the two systems:

- **Technology**. The most straightforward challenge was the merging of database technologies. The team chose a standard database technology for the new integrated system.

- **History**. More perplexing was what to do about the historical data collected in each of the systems. Was the new system just for future customers, or were all existing customers to be included in the newly integrated system as well? The team decided to include all existing customers as well as future customers. This will make the integration effort more difficult. Now, there would be a need to go back and convert old data to the new system. Even though there was a price to pay for including existing customers in the integrated database, the organization felt it was worth the effort.

- **Merge process**. The greatest challenge came in determining exactly how to merge the systems. The database designer for each of the systems was long gone, and the designers had never done any collaboration. The original designers never thought their systems would be merged.

Structured data

The committee started with a comparison of the simple layout of the data for both systems.

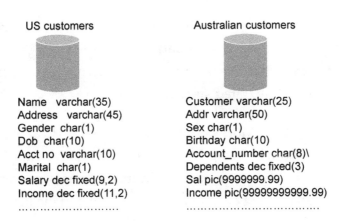

US customers	Australian customers
Name varchar(35)	Customer varchar(25)
Address varchar(45)	Addr varchar(50)
Gender char(1)	Sex char(1)
Dob char(10)	Birthday char(10)
Acct no varchar(10)	Account_number char(8)\
Marital char(1)	Dependents dec fixed(3)
Salary dec fixed(9,2)	Sal pic(9999999.99)
Income dec fixed(11,2)	Income pic(99999999999.99)

Figure 12-2. The layouts were placed side by side.

The first decision made by the committee was to standardize names. The names of the two files to be integrated were similar yet different. So, the team created their own set of names for the integrated environment. But naming conventions were just the starting point for the merger of the two systems.

The second observation was that there was data in the US database that wasn't in the Australian database and vice versa. So the team decided that when merging data, the attribute would be marked with "unknown" if there was no source for the data. In other words, if an attribute existed in the US database, such as Marital in the figure, this attribute would contain the value "unknown" when entering Australian data. There were a lot of other decisions to be made about how to merge the two files.

US customers

Name
Address
Gender m,f
Dob July 99,9999
Acct no 99-CCC99
Marital m/s/d/w
Salary US dollars
Income US dollars

....

Australian customers

Customer
Addr
Sex 1,0
Birthday yyyy/mm/dd
Account_number CCCC999999
Dependents
Sal Aus dollars
Income Aus dollars

....

Figure 12-3. The encoding, denomination, and format of the data are different.

One of the differences in the data was the encoding for gender. In the US, the encoding was m,f and in Australia the encoding was 1,0. So the team decided that in the integrated database, encoding would be uniformly m,f. This means that when adding data from the Australian database, that 1,0 will be converted to m,f.

Another resolution was the format of date of birth. The two databases used different formats. The team chose the Australian format for the integrated database. So the format of the US date of birth will be converted to the Australian format when loading US data.

A third difference was the format of the account number. It was simple enough to choose the integrated database account number format. However, some accounts existed in both countries. There weren't many, but a few people had accounts in both databases. Not always knowing if the same people owned the accounts with the same account numbers added to this complexity. In one account, the name was J A Smith and in another, James A Smith. It was unclear if this was the same person. Simply looking at address was not a clear indication of identification. Mr. Smith may have established an account in one address, and then moved and established another account in a different address.

That team decided that if the address for the accounts was the same, then Mr. Smith's identification was established. But if the name was the same or similar, and if there were two different addresses for the person, then we would contact the person by email to confirm identity. If there was no response by email, we would call the person.

If there was no final resolution as to the actual owner of the account, we would create two accounts even though the accounts might be for the same person. In doing so, the system designers ensured that no customer would be inadvertently left out. Although this process might lead to some data integrity issues, the number would be very small.

Fortunately, there were only a handful of these accounts, so the manual effort of mailing and using the telephone was limited in scope.

Another challenge between the two files was agreeing on currency. The US uses US dollars and Australia uses Australian dollars. The team decided to keep records in US dollars. For this purpose, a mathematical conversion will convert Australian dollars into American dollars.

But a mere calculation of exchange rates was not sufficient. The problem was that the exchange rate between the two currencies was constantly changing. So the team also decided to store the date of the exchange rate conversion. This way, a recalculation could be done for the present values of the exchange rate, if needed.

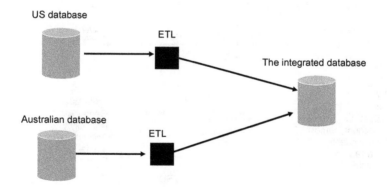

Figure 12-4. The resulting architectural rendering of the conversion and integration of different systems.

The most difficult part of integrating the two systems was in finding overlapping data. The team would perform in this order: an account search, a names analysis, an email contact, and a telephone call.

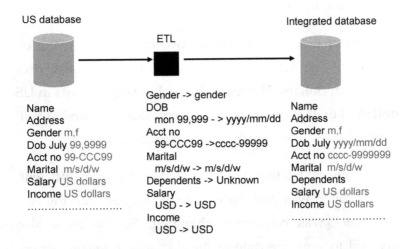

Figure 12-5. The transformation programs in ETL for the US data to be transformed into integrated data.

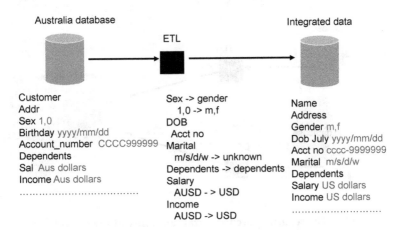

Figure 12-6. The transformation programs in ETL for the Australia data to be transformed into integrated data.

The transformation process resulted from a coordinated and unified effort. There was the:

- Manual work required to rectify accounts
- The ETL work to transform existing data
- The programs that needed to feed the new customers into the integrated systems

The transformation's net result was a database representing the organization's data. Now management could have a consolidated view of data.

Textual data

For several reasons, integrating and incorporating textual data is simpler. The first reason is that no existing systems had already collected textual data. As a consequence, there was no conversion of existing data. The second reason for the simplicity is that there is now Textual ETL technology specifically designed to capture and integrate textual data.

The first step was the capture and ingestion of the text. After text ingestion, select the appropriate taxonomies for processing the text. The taxonomies could:

- Be built internally
- Be purchased commercially from someone like Wand, Inc

- Be acquired from the organization that sells Textual ETL

We then load the most appropriate taxonomies into textual ETL. Now Textual ETL is ready for processing.

The next step is to process the documents through Textual ETL. If there are many documents, we can process the documents in parallel.

The final step is creating the database made up of the text that has been read.

Once the text was in the form of a database, thousands of records could be accessed and analyzed simultaneously.

Summary

After integrating structured and textual data, the data forms a foundation for analyzing data across the entire organization.

CHAPTER 13

Integration Considerations

Plan

The first option for full data integration begins with planning. You need to know what you want before you can ask for it. There are many existing data models for a data warehouse. There are industry standards. You do not need to rebuild the wheel! It already exists...it is round and it rolls! You may need to add chrome to the spokes to get what you need, but you need to know that first. Once you understand what data you need at the end, create the formats for the ending requirements of pre-cleaned data. These JSON, XML, or other industry-standard formats help your integrators with well-defined data export templates.

Building these formats requires upper-level data governance teams. These teams consist of employees who are subject matter experts in their silos and who also have or want experience with other silos. These cross-trained employees help with this high-level planning.

Now, pass these data import templates to each system's handlers. Have subject matter experts in each silo, as part of that department's data governance team, work with developers or database administrators to properly export the data into the new format.

Finally, before you allow the creation of any new systems or purchase of any new ones, talk directly with the vendors or developers and ensure they can export the data according to your pre-cleaned format. When the final exports are part of the system requirements, the developers or system providers have an end goal requirement that they will have to achieve to earn your business. We need to bring on new systems with the understanding of organization-wide goals as well as the requirements of the departmental task. If you make this goal an "add-on", it might stay on the "in-progress" list.

Educate

Humans value what they know and downgrade the work of other parts of the organization. We each think we are crucial and worth more than we are because we don't see or understand another department's job. Ignorance kills cooperation. Your employees need to see past their departments. We need to train them on how each part of the organization, from the janitors to the CEO, from HR to

Advertising, all add value. They should see how their position adds value to the other departments dependent on them and vice versa. This takes time, but must be part of the planning and organization culture if we want each employee to use integrated data.

Cross-training helps with data integration. Specialization is important to perform a specific task like accounting, finance, and manufacturing, but none of these functions work in a vacuum. Show your employees how they are part of the bigger picture. They need to be part of that bigger picture.

Your employees should be on a series of cross-functional teams. For example, part of each week should be spent interacting with other departments or being part of an organization's data governance team or information systems steering committee.

These cross-functional teams also build a corporate culture of cooperation instead of internal competition. New ideas and ways to use integrated data to create competitive advantages happen within these teams. They happen at the water cooler. They rarely happen from the middle and upper management. They cannot happen in the vacuum of a functional silo.

As employees get to know the organization's systems better, they become subject matter experts within their silos. These employees see what data is missing, yet needed, to do their jobs better. By adding them to the data governance teams, they can explain what the entered data actually means and explain the full metadata meaning to people outside of their functional area. They can also see where missing data might be able to be obtained through other departmental systems. The more employees see what data is available to them, the better they will be able to do their jobs, and easier it will be to put well-defined curated data into your data integration plan.

Management support

Top leadership needs to support and fund data integration. Although all of the data comes from the bottom systems of record, Point of Sale systems, automatic garage systems, call centers, Airplane Black Boxes, ERPs, and EMRs, the direction and budgets must come from the top with full definitions and budgets supporting expectations. You get what you pay for...so put your money behind integration. Without top-level support and endorsement, integration will continue to be hated. Data integration works best as a top-down approach.

Index

www.ingramcontent.com/pod-product-compliance
Lightning Source LLC
Chambersburg PA
CBHW071253050326
40690CB00011B/2377